# "Bringing in Cash on Pinterest: A Step-by-Step Guide"

## Introduction:

Welcome to the transformative realm of Pinterest, where creativity and commerce converge to offer an unprecedented opportunity for financial empowerment. In the ever-evolving digital sphere, platforms like Pinterest have redefined how individuals and businesses alike can harness the potential of social media to generate income.

"Bringing in Cash on Pinterest: A Step-by-Step Guide" is your comprehensive manual designed to unlock the full potential of this vibrant visual platform. Whether you're a budding entrepreneur, a seasoned marketer, a content creator, or someone eager to explore new avenues for monetary gain, this guide is tailored to equip you with the essential insights, strategies, and actionable steps needed to thrive in the realm of Pinterest monetization.

From deciphering the intricacies of Pinterest's algorithm to crafting engaging and marketable content, this guide will delve into the art of creating material that captivates your audience, optimizing for maximum visibility, and implementing effective monetization techniques. Uncover the strategies for driving traffic, converting leads, and transforming your Pinterest presence into a sustainable source of income.

Through a meticulously detailed approach, incorporating practical tips, real-world case studies, and actionable advice, this guide endeavours to empower you with the confidence and expertise required to navigate Pinterest's diverse landscape proficiently. Embrace the opportunity to monetize your passions, showcase your offerings, and embark on a journey toward financial success in the visually immersive world of Pinterest.

# INDEX

Here are 20 actionable ways to bring in cash on Pinterest:

1. **Create Compelling Pins:** Design visually appealing and informative pins using high-quality images and engaging text to capture attention.

2. **Optimize Pin Descriptions:** Write keyword-rich descriptions for your pins to improve discoverability in Pinterest search results and attract more viewers.

3. **Join Group Boards:** Collaborate with other users by joining relevant group boards to expand your reach and increase the visibility of your pins.

4. **Pin Consistently:** Maintain a consistent pinning schedule to keep your audience engaged and improve your chances of being seen on Pinterest.

5. **Utilize Rich Pins:** Enable rich pins (such as product, recipe, or article pins) to provide additional information directly on the pin, making it more valuable and enticing for users.

6. **Focus on SEO:** Optimize your profile and boards for search engines by using relevant keywords in your board titles, descriptions, and profile bio.

7. **Create How-To Guides or Tutorials:** Share valuable content in the form of step-by-step guides or tutorials that showcase your expertise and drive traffic to your website or products.

8. **Promote Affiliate Products:** Incorporate affiliate links into your pins to earn commissions when users make purchases through your recommendations.

9. **Offer Exclusive Deals or Coupons:** Create pins that highlight special offers, discounts, or coupons to entice Pinterest users to engage and make purchases.

10. **Sell Products Directly:** Utilize Pinterest's shopping features to showcase and sell your products directly through Buyable Pins or linking to your online store.

11. **Host Contests or Giveaways:** Organize contests or giveaways to encourage engagement, increase your reach, and attract new followers.

12. **Collaborate with Influencers:** Partner with influencers or other businesses in your niche for collaborations, joint boards, or sponsored content to reach a broader audience.

13. **Use Pinterest Ads:** Invest in promoted pins to reach a targeted audience and increase the visibility of your content.

14. **Create Educational Content:** Share informative and educational content related to your niche to establish authority and build trust with your audience.

15. **Offer Consultation or Services:** Promote your services or expertise by creating pins that showcase what you offer and how it benefits potential clients.

16. **Curate Curiosity Boards:** Create boards that pique interest and curiosity, driving users to explore and engage with your content.

17. **Share User-Generated Content:** Encourage users to share their experiences with your products or services and feature their content on your boards.

18. **Cross-Promote on Other Platforms:** Share your pins on other social media platforms, blogs, or websites to drive traffic back to your Pinterest account.

19. **Create Seasonal or Holiday Boards:** Capitalize on seasonal trends or holidays by creating themed boards and pins to attract seasonal shoppers.

20. **Track Analytics and Optimize:** Monitor Pinterest analytics to understand what content performs best and use this data to refine your strategies for better results.

By implementing these strategies consistently and adapting them to suit your specific audience and niche, you can effectively leverage Pinterest's potential to bring in cash and grow your online presence.

# Chapter -1

1. **Create Compelling Pins:** Design visually appealing and informative pins using high-quality images and engaging text to capture attention.

Creating compelling pins on Pinterest is a pivotal aspect of harnessing the platform's potential to captivate audiences and drive engagement. These pins serve as the visual gateway to your content, products, or services, making them crucial in attracting and retaining user attention. Crafting visually appealing, informative, and high-quality pins is an art form that requires strategic design and compelling content to stand out in the sea of digital imagery.

Firstly, the visual element of a pin is fundamental. High-quality images are the cornerstone of an attention-grabbing pin. The use of high-resolution photos that are clear, vibrant, and well-composed significantly enhances the visual appeal. Whether showcasing a product, sharing a recipe, or presenting an idea, the image should be the focal point, drawing the viewer in and evoking interest.

Additionally, the text overlay on the pin plays a crucial role in conveying information and enticing users to take action. The engaging text should complement the visual component, providing context, highlighting key points, or prompting the viewer to learn more. It's essential to use concise and impactful wording that is easily readable and complements the overall aesthetic without overshadowing the image.

Moreover, incorporating branding elements, such as logos or consistent colour schemes, helps establish brand recognition and reinforces the pin's association with your content or business. Consistency in branding across pins cultivates a cohesive and recognizable identity, enhancing your brand's visibility and recall among Pinterest users.

The layout and design of the pin should be visually appealing and user-friendly. Strategic placement of text, use of white space, and balanced composition contribute to the overall attractiveness and readability of the pin. Experimenting with different layouts, fonts, and graphic elements can add variety while maintaining coherence within your pin designs.

Understanding the preferences and interests of your target audience is pivotal. Tailoring pin designs to resonate with their tastes, preferences, and aspirations increases the likelihood of engagement and encourages users to explore further. Researching trending topics, styles, and themes within your niche can provide valuable insights into creating pins that align with current interests.

Furthermore, the timing of pinning is crucial for maximizing visibility and engagement. Identifying peak times when your target audience is most active on Pinterest can amplify the reach of your pins. Scheduling pins at optimal times and consistently sharing content ensures a steady flow of engagement and exposure.

Utilizing Pinterest's features, such as rich pins or video pins, can diversify your content and appeal to different user preferences. Rich pins offer additional information directly on the pin, while video pins provide an interactive and dynamic way to engage users, both enhancing the overall spinnability and shareability of your content.

In conclusion, crafting compelling pins on Pinterest requires a strategic fusion of visually captivating imagery, engaging text, brand consistency, user-centric design, and an understanding of audience preferences. By dedicating time and effort to creating pins that resonate with your target audience, you can effectively leverage Pinterest as a powerful platform to attract attention, drive engagement, and ultimately achieve your goals, whether it's increasing website traffic, promoting products, or building brand awareness.

# Chapter - 2

2. **Optimize Pin Descriptions:** Write keyword-rich descriptions for your pins to improve discoverability in Pinterest search results and attract more viewers.

Optimizing pin descriptions on Pinterest is a crucial aspect of enhancing discoverability, increasing visibility, and attracting a larger audience to your content. Crafting keyword-rich descriptions empowers your pins to rank higher in Pinterest's search results, ensuring they reach the right audience at the right time. An effective pin description serves as a gateway, providing context, and information, and enticing users to engage further.

Understanding the significance of keywords is foundational in creating impactful pin descriptions. Keywords are terms or phrases that users are likely to search for when looking for specific content. Integrating relevant keywords organically within your pin descriptions enables Pinterest's algorithm to recognize and categorize your pins accurately.

Begin by conducting thorough keyword research to identify phrases or terms that are pertinent to your content or business. Utilize tools like Pinterest's own search bar, Google's Keyword Planner, or third-party keyword research tools to uncover popular search queries within your niche. Selecting a mix of broad and specific keywords relevant to your content allows you to target a wider audience while catering to more niche interests.

When writing pin descriptions, ensure they are informative, concise, and engaging. Aim to incorporate relevant keywords naturally within the text without compromising readability or coherence. An effective description not only includes keywords but also provides valuable information, enticing users to click through to your content, website, or product.

Furthermore, using compelling language that sparks curiosity or emotion can pique interest and encourage users to explore further. Address the audience directly, highlight unique selling points, or convey a compelling call-to-action within the description to prompt engagement.

Maintain consistency in tone, voice, and style across your pin descriptions to reinforce your brand identity and establish a cohesive presence on Pinterest. This consistency helps users recognize your content amidst the multitude of pins, fostering trust and familiarity.

Consider the length of your pin descriptions as well. Pinterest allows for more extensive descriptions, but it's essential to strike a balance between providing enough information and not overwhelming users with excessive text. Aim for descriptions that offer value and clarity without being excessively long.

Moreover, optimize your pin descriptions for both Pinterest's search engine and users. While keywords are vital for search visibility, ensure that the descriptions remain user-friendly and engaging. Catering to the user's intent and providing valuable insights or solutions increases the likelihood of engagement and encourages users to take action.

Utilize hashtags strategically within your pin descriptions. Hashtags can amplify your pin's reach beyond your followers and aid in categorizing content. Incorporate relevant hashtags that align with your content or industry, keeping them concise and focused to maximize their effectiveness.

Regularly review and refine your pin descriptions based on performance metrics and user engagement. Monitoring Pinterest analytics provides valuable insights into which keywords, descriptions, or content types resonate best with your audience. This data-driven approach allows for continuous optimization and refinement of your pin descriptions to enhance their effectiveness.

In conclusion, optimizing pin descriptions on Pinterest involves meticulous keyword research, strategic integration of keywords, compelling and informative content, consistent branding, a user-centric approach, and continuous refinement based on analytics. By mastering the art of crafting keyword-rich descriptions that resonate with your target audience, you can significantly improve your pins' discoverability, attract more viewers, and ultimately drive engagement and success on the platform.

# Chapter - 3

3. **Join Group Boards:** Collaborate with other users by joining relevant group boards to expand your reach and increase the visibility of your pins.

Joining group boards on Pinterest is a strategic move to expand your reach, increase visibility, and enhance the exposure of your pins. These collaborative boards bring together like-minded individuals or businesses sharing a common interest or niche, offering a valuable opportunity to engage with a broader audience beyond your followers and amplify the visibility of your content.

Finding and joining relevant group boards is a key step in leveraging the collective audience of these communities. Start by conducting searches within Pinterest or using third-party websites that curate lists of group boards. Look for boards that align with your niche, have an engaged audience, and allow contributors to share content regularly.

When requesting to join group boards, it's essential to follow the board's guidelines and rules. Some boards have specific criteria for joining, such as following the board owner, engaging with existing content, or sending a request via email. Personalizing your request and demonstrating your commitment to contributing value to the board can increase the likelihood of being accepted as a contributor.

Upon gaining access to group boards, maintain active participation by consistently sharing high-quality, relevant content that aligns with the board's theme. Adhere to the board's rules regarding pin frequency and content guidelines to foster a positive collaborative environment.

Collaboration within group boards offers a multitude of benefits. Firstly, it extends your reach beyond your followers, exposing your content to a wider and potentially more diverse audience interested in the specific niche of the board. This increased visibility can result in higher engagement rates, including repins, likes, and click-throughs to your profile or website.

Moreover, being part of group boards facilitates networking and interaction with other contributors who share similar interests or expertise. Engaging with fellow contributors by repinning, liking, or commenting on their content can foster meaningful connections, potentially leading to collaborations, cross-promotion opportunities, or increased exposure within their networks.

Additionally, group boards often enjoy higher visibility within Pinterest's algorithm, as they tend to be more active and receive increased engagement due to multiple contributors sharing content. This increased activity can positively impact the visibility and performance of your pins within these boards.

It's crucial to maintain a balance between sharing your content and repinning others' content within group boards. Aim for a healthy mix of your original pins and repins that resonate with the board's theme to keep the content fresh and diverse. Engaging with others' content not only fosters a sense of community but also encourages reciprocity in sharing your content.

Regularly assess the performance of your pins within group boards using Pinterest analytics. Monitor metrics such as impressions, clicks, and engagement rates to gauge the effectiveness of your contributions. Analyzing these insights helps identify the types of content that resonate best with the board's audience, allowing for strategic adjustments and optimization of your pinning strategy.

As with any collaborative platform, it's important to maintain professionalism, respect the board's guidelines, and contribute value to the community. Avoid spamming the board with excessive self-promotion or irrelevant content, as this can detract from the collaborative spirit and negatively impact your reputation within the group.

In conclusion, joining relevant group boards on Pinterest presents an opportunity to expand your reach, increase visibility, and engage with a wider audience within your niche. Strategic participation in these communities by sharing valuable content, fostering connections with fellow contributors, and adhering to board guidelines can significantly enhance the exposure and performance of your pins. Leveraging the collective audience and collaborative nature of group boards can be a powerful strategy to grow your presence and achieve success on Pinterest.

# Chapter - 4

4. **Pin Consistently:** Maintain a consistent pinning schedule to keep your audience engaged and improve your chances of being seen on Pinterest.

Consistency in pinning plays a pivotal role in sustaining audience engagement, maximizing visibility, and establishing a strong presence on Pinterest. Maintaining a regular and consistent pinning schedule is essential for reaching and retaining your audience's attention amidst the vast array of content circulating on the platform. A consistent presence not only keeps your audience engaged but also increases the likelihood of your content being seen by a broader audience.

Establishing a consistent pinning schedule begins with understanding your audience's behaviour and preferences. Analyze Pinterest analytics to identify peak activity times when your audience is most active and engaged. This data-driven approach allows you to schedule pins strategically, ensuring they are seen by a larger audience during optimal times.

Developing a content calendar or pinning schedule helps maintain consistency in your pinning strategy. Plan and organize your pins in advance, considering various factors such as content type, themes, and the frequency of pinning. This structured approach ensures a steady flow of content without overwhelming your audience with a barrage of pins or periods of inactivity.

Maintaining consistency does not solely entail quantity; quality is equally crucial. Focus on creating high-quality, visually appealing pins that resonate with your audience and align with their interests. Investing time in crafting compelling content ensures that each pin contributes meaningfully to your overall Pinterest strategy.

Utilize scheduling tools or Pinterest's native scheduler to automate the posting of pins at predetermined times. These tools allow you to maintain consistency even during periods when manual pinning might not be feasible, ensuring a consistent flow of content to your audience.

Diversifying the types of content you pin is also essential in maintaining audience interest and engagement. Experiment with various formats, such as static images, video pins, carousel pins, or story pins, to cater to different preferences within your audience. Additionally, vary the content by incorporating a mix of original content and curated pins to provide a well-rounded and engaging experience for your audience.

Consistency extends beyond pin frequency to encompass maintaining a cohesive visual aesthetic and brand identity across your pins and boards. Consistent branding elements, such as colour schemes, fonts, and logos, create a recognisable and unified presence on Pinterest, reinforcing your brand identity and enhancing overall user experience.

Engage with your audience regularly by responding to comments, messages, or interactions on your pins. Building a rapport with your audience fosters a sense of community and loyalty, encouraging continued engagement and interaction with your content.

While consistency is vital, it's essential to strike a balance and avoid overwhelming your audience with excessive pinning. Aim for a consistent schedule that delivers valuable and relevant content without inundating users with an excessive number of pins in a short timeframe.

Regularly assess the performance of your pins using Pinterest analytics to evaluate the impact of your consistency efforts. Analyze metrics such as impressions, engagements, click-through rates, and follower growth to gain insights into which pins resonate best with your audience. Adjust your pinning strategy based on these insights to optimize performance further.

Moreover, stay updated with Pinterest trends, algorithm changes, and best practices to adapt your pinning strategy accordingly. Embracing new features or trends can keep your content fresh and appealing to your audience, enhancing engagement and visibility.

In conclusion, maintaining a consistent pinning schedule on Pinterest is paramount for sustaining audience engagement, maximizing visibility, and establishing a strong and enduring presence on the platform. By understanding your audience, planning a structured content calendar, focusing on quality content creation, maintaining brand consistency, and engaging regularly, you can effectively leverage consistency as a cornerstone of your Pinterest strategy. Consistent, strategic pinning is a powerful tool for cultivating a loyal audience, increasing visibility, and achieving success on Pinterest.

# Chapter - 5

5. **Utilize Rich Pins:** Enable rich pins (such as product, recipe, or article pins) to provide additional information directly on the pin, making it more valuable and enticing for users.

Utilizing rich pins on Pinterest is a powerful strategy to enhance the value, engagement, and utility of your pins. These specialized pins, including product, recipe, and article pins, offer additional contextual information directly within the pin itself, enriching the user experience and providing valuable details that entice users to engage further.

There are several types of rich pins, each tailored to specific content categories, allowing creators, businesses, and publishers to showcase their offerings more effectively:

1. **Product Pins:** Product pins enable businesses to display real-time pricing, availability, and direct links to purchase the featured product. By syncing with the website's metadata, these pins dynamically update information like pricing, availability, and where to buy the product, providing users with current and actionable details.

2. **Recipe Pins:** Recipe pins provide users with detailed ingredients, cooking times, serving sizes, and step-by-step instructions directly on the pin. These rich pins are a boon for food bloggers, chefs, or culinary enthusiasts, offering a glimpse into the recipe without requiring users to navigate away from Pinterest.

3. **Article Pins:** Article pins offer a snapshot of informative articles, blog posts, or news pieces, presenting the headline, author, and a brief description within the pin. This format appeals to publishers, bloggers, or content creators aiming to attract readership by providing a sneak peek into the content's essence.

Enabling rich pins involves incorporating metadata markup on your website, ensuring that Pinterest can extract and display the additional information associated with each pin. This process typically involves adding specific Open Graph or Schema.org markup to the backend of your website, ensuring that the relevant data is available for Pinterest to showcase within rich pins.

The value of rich pins lies in their ability to provide users with immediate, relevant information without requiring them to click through to the website. This convenience enhances the user experience, increasing engagement and fostering a stronger connection between users and content creators or businesses.

For businesses, product pins offer a streamlined shopping experience by showcasing real-time pricing and availability, encouraging users to make informed purchase decisions directly from the pin. This direct link to the product significantly reduces friction in the buyer's journey, increasing the likelihood of conversions and sales.

Similarly, recipe pins cater to food enthusiasts by offering comprehensive details within the pin itself, eliminating the need to navigate to external websites for cooking instructions or ingredient lists. Users can save, share, and explore recipes seamlessly without disrupting their browsing experience.

Article pins cater to publishers and content creators by providing a glimpse into the article's content, enticing users to click through to read the full piece. This format aids in attracting readership, increasing traffic to websites, and fostering engagement with informative or compelling content.

Moreover, rich pins often enjoy greater visibility and engagement on Pinterest due to their enhanced informational value. Pinterest's algorithm tends to favour content that provides valuable, detailed information, increasing the likelihood of rich pins being recommended and surfaced to users.

Regularly monitoring the performance of rich pins through Pinterest analytics is crucial. Analyze metrics such as impressions, clicks, saves, and engagement rates to assess the effectiveness of rich pins in driving traffic, conversions, or user engagement. Use these insights to refine pinning strategies and optimize rich pin content for better performance.

In conclusion, leveraging rich pins on Pinterest is a strategic approach to enriching content, enhancing user experience, and driving engagement. By incorporating real-time information, detailed instructions, or sneak peeks directly within the pins, content creators, publishers, and businesses can captivate audiences, encourage interaction, and streamline user journeys. Enabling rich pins not only adds value to the user experience but also boosts visibility and engagement, making them a valuable asset in any comprehensive Pinterest marketing strategy.

# Chapter- 6

6. **Focus on SEO:** Optimize your profile and boards for search engines by using relevant keywords in your board titles, descriptions, and profile bio.

Focusing on Search Engine Optimization (SEO) within your Pinterest profile and boards is a crucial strategy to enhance discoverability, improve search rankings, and attract a targeted audience interested in your content or products. Optimizing your profile involves strategic use of relevant keywords in board titles, descriptions, and your profile bio, ensuring that your content is easily found by users searching for specific topics or themes.

Starting with your profile bio, crafting a concise and keyword-rich description is fundamental. This brief introduction serves as a snapshot of your brand, content, or business. Incorporating relevant keywords related to your niche or offerings within the bio improves the likelihood of your profile appearing in search results when users look for specific topics or categories. Additionally, including a call-to-action or links to your website can further encourage engagement and drive traffic to your desired destination.

Optimizing board titles and descriptions is equally essential. Board titles should be descriptive and contain targeted keywords that accurately represent the board's content. Aim to use specific and relevant keywords that align with your content strategy to increase the likelihood of your boards ranking higher in Pinterest's search results.

Moreover, board descriptions offer an opportunity to provide more context and detail about the board's content. Incorporating a mix of primary and secondary keywords within these descriptions helps Pinterest's algorithm understand the board's relevance to specific search queries. By using natural language and informative descriptions, you can attract users interested in the topics or themes represented by your boards.

A key aspect of effective SEO on Pinterest is conducting thorough keyword research to identify relevant and high-performing keywords within your niche. Utilize Pinterest's search bar, keyword research tools, or external platforms like Google Keyword Planner to explore popular search queries, trending topics, or niche-specific keywords. Incorporate these keywords strategically into your profile, board titles, and descriptions to optimize for search visibility.

Consistency in using keywords across your profile and boards is crucial for reinforcing your content's relevance and improving discoverability. Aligning your content with targeted keywords helps users find your profile and boards when searching for specific topics, increasing the chances of engagement and followership.

Furthermore, categorizing your boards correctly is essential for SEO. Assigning each board to the most relevant category ensures that your content appears in the appropriate sections of Pinterest's search results, improving its visibility to users interested in those specific categories.

Regularly updating and refreshing your profile, board titles, and descriptions with relevant keywords is essential for maintaining search visibility and staying relevant within your niche. Keeping abreast of trending topics, evolving search trends, and user preferences allows you to adapt and optimize your content strategy accordingly.

Leveraging Pinterest's analytics tools is imperative to gauge the effectiveness of your SEO efforts. Monitor metrics such as impressions, clicks, and engagement rates attributed to specific keywords or boards. Analyzing this data provides insights into which keywords or boards perform best, enabling you to refine your SEO strategy for better results.

In conclusion, focusing on SEO within your Pinterest profile and boards involves strategic keyword integration, crafting informative and relevant descriptions, and maintaining consistency in content optimization. By incorporating targeted keywords, providing valuable context, and aligning your content with user search intent, you can significantly improve the discoverability of your profile and boards. A well-optimized Pinterest presence not only enhances search visibility but also attracts a relevant audience interested in your content, ultimately contributing to increased engagement and success on the platform.

# Chapter - 7

7. **Create How-To Guides or Tutorials:** Share valuable content in the form of step-by-step guides or tutorials that showcase your expertise and drive traffic to your website or products.

Creating how-to guides or tutorials on Pinterest is a powerful strategy to provide valuable, informative content that showcases your expertise, engages your audience, and drives traffic to your website or products. These step-by-step guides serve as a means to offer users practical solutions, instructions, or insights into various topics, establishing credibility and authority within your niche.

The essence of a successful how-to guide lies in addressing the needs, interests, or pain points of your target audience. Identify topics or subjects relevant to your expertise, industry, or the interests of your audience. Whether it's DIY projects, educational tutorials, cooking recipes, or instructional content, choose topics that resonate with your audience and align with your brand or offerings.

When creating a how-to guide, structure it in a clear, sequential format that guides users through each step or process. Begin with a compelling introduction that outlines the purpose and benefits of following the guide. Break down the content into easy-to-follow steps or sections, accompanied by descriptive text, visuals, infographics, or videos to enhance comprehension and engagement.

Visual elements, such as high-quality images or videos, play a pivotal role in elucidating each step of the guide. Incorporate visuals that complement the written instructions, providing clarity and aiding users in understanding and following the process more effectively. Utilize Pinterest's image-focused platform to showcase visually appealing content that stands out and attracts users' attention.

Furthermore, optimize your how-to guides for Pinterest by creating pinnable images or graphics that serve as a visual representation of the guide. Design eye-catching pins that convey the essence of the guide, entice users to click through, and encourage engagement. Incorporate text overlay, compelling visuals, and branding elements to make the pin visually appealing and shareable.

Incorporate relevant keywords in the pin's title, description, and alt text to improve searchability and increase the chances of your content being discovered by users searching for related topics. Including a clear and concise call-to-action within the pin description encourages users to engage further, directing them to your website, blog post, or product page for more information or to complete a desired action.

Moreover, consider repurposing or repackaging your existing content into comprehensive how-to guides. Convert blog posts, video tutorials, or instructional content into a visually appealing format suitable for Pinterest. Repurposing content not only maximizes its reach but also allows you to leverage existing resources and capitalize on proven content that resonates with your audience.

Promoting your how-to guides across various platforms and channels can amplify their reach and engagement. Share your guides on other social media platforms, in newsletters, or through collaborations with influencers or relevant communities. Cross-promotion encourages wider exposure and increases the likelihood of driving traffic back to your website or products.

Regularly track the performance of your how-to guides using Pinterest analytics to gain insights into their effectiveness. Monitor metrics such as impressions, click-through rates, saves, and engagement to assess user response and guide future content strategies. Analyzing this data helps in understanding which types of guides or topics resonate best with your audience, enabling you to refine and optimize your content creation approach.

In conclusion, creating how-to guides or tutorials on Pinterest is a valuable approach to providing informative, engaging content that showcases your expertise and drives traffic to your website or products. By offering step-by-step instructions, visual aids, and shareable content, you can establish credibility, engage your audience, and attract users interested in your niche. Leveraging

Pinterest's visual platform to showcase your guides effectively can significantly enhance your online presence, increase engagement, and ultimately drive meaningful traffic and conversions to your desired destinations.

# Chapter - 8

8. **Promote Affiliate Products:** Incorporate affiliate links into your pins to earn commissions when users make purchases through your recommendations.

Promoting affiliate products on Pinterest is a lucrative strategy for earning commissions by leveraging the platform's visual appeal and engaging content. By incorporating affiliate links into your pins, you have the opportunity to earn commissions when users make purchases through the products or services you recommend.

Affiliate marketing on Pinterest involves partnering with affiliate programs or networks that offer commissions for sales generated through your referral links. These programs provide unique affiliate links that track users' interactions and purchases, allowing you to earn a percentage of the sale as a commission.

To start, select affiliate programs or networks that align with your niche, interests, or the preferences of your audience. Research reputable and relevant affiliate programs that offer products or services that resonate with your audience's needs or preferences. Ensure that the affiliate products you choose are of high quality, align with your brand ethos, and are genuinely beneficial to your audience.

Create visually appealing and engaging pins that feature the affiliate products you wish to promote. Design eye-catching graphics or images that showcase the products authentically and appealingly. Incorporate compelling text overlays or descriptions that highlight the product's features, benefits, and value proposition to entice users to explore further.

When sharing affiliate product pins, disclose your affiliate relationship transparently and ethically. Pinterest requires users to disclose any paid or sponsored content, including affiliate links, to maintain transparency and trust with the audience. Include clear and conspicuous disclosures, such as "#ad," "affiliate link," or "paid partnership," to ensure compliance with Pinterest's guidelines and ethical practices.

Strategically place affiliate product pins across relevant boards on your profile to maximize visibility and exposure. Create dedicated boards specifically for affiliate products or seamlessly integrate them into boards related to your niche or audience interests. Organize pins in a visually appealing and user-friendly manner to enhance the browsing experience.

Write compelling pin descriptions that provide valuable information, answer potential questions, and encourage users to take action. Incorporate relevant keywords within the pin descriptions to improve discoverability and increase the chances of your pins being found by users searching for related products or topics.

Consider diversifying your affiliate product pins by showcasing various products, product reviews, comparisons, or curated lists that cater to different preferences within your audience. Providing diverse and informative content increases the chances of resonating with a wider audience and encouraging click-throughs to affiliate product pages.

Monitor the performance of your affiliate product pins using Pinterest analytics to gain insights into their effectiveness. Track metrics such as impressions, clicks, saves, and conversion rates to assess the engagement levels and success of your affiliate marketing efforts. Analyze this data to understand which products or pins perform best and refine your strategy accordingly.

Engage with your audience by responding to comments, inquiries, or feedback related to the affiliate products you promote. Building rapport and trust with your audience fosters a sense of authenticity and credibility, encouraging users to consider and trust your product recommendations.

Additionally, consider creating content that adds value and complements the affiliate products you promote. Craft blog posts, tutorials, or reviews that provide in-depth information, insights, or recommendations related to the products. Use Pinterest to drive traffic to these informative resources, increasing the chances of users making informed purchasing decisions.

Regularly review and update your affiliate marketing strategy on Pinterest to adapt to changing trends, audience preferences, or new affiliate opportunities. Stay informed about new products, promotions, or seasonal offers to capitalize on timely opportunities to promote affiliate products effectively.

In conclusion, promoting affiliate products on Pinterest offers a promising avenue for earning commissions by leveraging the platform's visual appeal and engaging content. By creating visually captivating pins, strategically sharing affiliate products, disclosing affiliations transparently, and providing valuable content, you can effectively monetize your Pinterest presence and drive commissions through user engagement and product recommendations. Leveraging Pinterest's visual platform to showcase affiliate products can be a rewarding strategy when executed thoughtfully, ethically, and in alignment with your audience's interests and preferences.

# Chapter - 9

9. **Offer Exclusive Deals or Coupons:** Create pins that highlight special offers, discounts, or coupons to entice Pinterest users to engage and make purchases.

Offering exclusive deals or coupons on Pinterest is a strategic approach to engaging users, driving traffic, and boosting sales by showcasing special offers, discounts, or promotional deals. Creating pins that highlight exclusive deals or coupons entices Pinterest users, encouraging them to engage and make purchases while fostering a sense of urgency and value in their buying decisions.

To start, identify exclusive deals, discounts, or promotional offers that you can provide to your audience. These could include limited-time discounts, special promotions, coupon codes, bundled offers, or exclusive deals for Pinterest users. Tailor these offers to align with the preferences and needs of your target audience, ensuring they resonate and add value.

Design visually appealing and attention-grabbing pins that effectively showcase the exclusive deals or coupons you're offering.

Create eye-catching graphics, images, or videos that convey the offer, using compelling visuals and text overlays to communicate the value proposition of the deal. Incorporate persuasive messaging that emphasizes the exclusivity and benefits of the offer to entice users to take action.

When crafting pin descriptions for exclusive deals or coupons, focus on communicating the details of the offer concisely and clearly. Include relevant information such as discount percentages, promo codes, expiration dates, and any specific terms or conditions associated with the offer. Incorporating persuasive language that encourages users to "act now," "grab the offer," or "limited time only" instils a sense of urgency, prompting immediate action.

Ensure transparency and honesty in promoting exclusive deals or coupons on Pinterest. Disclose any terms, limitations, or restrictions associated with the offer to maintain trust and credibility with your audience. Transparency fosters a positive relationship with users and avoids any potential confusion or dissatisfaction.

Organize a dedicated board or multiple boards specifically showcasing exclusive deals, discounts, or coupons to make it easier for users to find and explore your promotional offers. Categorize these boards according to different offer types or themes, facilitating a seamless browsing experience for users interested in specific deals.

Regularly update and refresh your exclusive deals or coupons on Pinterest to keep the content relevant and engaging. Introduce new promotions, seasonal offers, or limited-time deals to maintain users' interest and encourage them to revisit your boards for fresh opportunities.

Pin the exclusive deal or coupon pins strategically across various relevant boards within your profile to maximize their visibility and exposure. Incorporate these pins into boards related to your niche, product categories, or specific interests of your audience to reach a wider user base interested in those topics.

Engage with your audience by responding to comments, inquiries, or feedback related to the exclusive deals or coupons you're offering. Actively participating in discussions or providing additional information fosters a sense of authenticity and trust, encouraging users to explore and avail themselves of your offers.

Leverage Pinterest's native features, such as Rich Pins or Buyable Pins, to enhance the visibility and functionality of your exclusive deals or coupons. Rich Pins provide additional information directly on the pin, while Buyable Pins allow users to make purchases directly through Pinterest, streamlining the buying process and increasing conversion rates.

Regularly monitor the performance of your exclusive deals or coupon pins using Pinterest analytics to assess their effectiveness. Track metrics such as impressions, clicks, saves, and conversion rates to understand user engagement and the success of your promotional offers. Analyzing this data helps in identifying which offers resonate best with your audience and refining your strategy for better results.

In conclusion, offering exclusive deals or coupons on Pinterest is a strategic approach to engaging users, driving traffic, and boosting sales by highlighting special offers or discounts. By creating visually appealing and persuasive pins, organizing dedicated boards, maintaining transparency, and actively engaging with users, you can effectively leverage Pinterest's platform to showcase enticing deals and encourage users to make purchases. Capitalizing on the visual nature of Pinterest and providing valuable exclusive offers tailored to your audience's interests can significantly enhance user engagement and drive conversions, ultimately contributing to the success of your promotional campaigns.

# Chapter-10

10. **Sell Products Directly:** Utilize Pinterest's shopping features to showcase and sell your products directly through Buyable Pins or linking to your online store.

Utilizing Pinterest's shopping features, such as Buyable Pins, presents a valuable opportunity to showcase and sell products directly to users, streamlining the buying process and leveraging the platform's visual appeal to drive sales. By incorporating these shopping functionalities, businesses can effectively showcase products, encourage purchases, and create a seamless shopping experience for Pinterest users.

To begin selling products directly on Pinterest, businesses need to have an online store or a platform where the products are available for purchase. Integration with Pinterest's shopping features enables the creation of Buyable Pins that allow users to make purchases without leaving the platform.

Setting up Buyable Pins involves partnering with e-commerce platforms or utilizing compatible tools that integrate with Pinterest, allowing for product catalogue synchronization and the creation of shoppable pins. Platforms like Shopify, BigCommerce, or

WooCommerce offer seamless integrations that enable businesses to sync their product listings with Pinterest.

Once integrated, businesses can create visually appealing and engaging Buyable Pins that showcase their products effectively. Design captivating images or graphics that highlight product features, aesthetics, and value propositions. Incorporate clear and concise text overlays that provide essential product information, pricing, and calls to action encouraging users to make purchases.

Utilize Pinterest's Product Pins, a type of Rich Pin, to enhance the shopping experience by displaying real-time pricing, availability, and direct links to the product page. Product Pins dynamically update information, ensuring users have access to current details, and making the buying process convenient and efficient.

Organize product pins within dedicated boards or across relevant boards to showcase different product categories, collections, or themes. Categorize and curate boards in a way that facilitates easy browsing and navigation for users interested in specific products or product lines.

Optimize product descriptions and titles with relevant keywords to improve search visibility and increase the likelihood of product discovery by users searching for related items. Incorporate descriptive and engaging text that highlights product benefits, unique features, and potential use cases to entice users to explore further and make a purchase.

Leverage Pinterest's audience targeting options and Promoted Pins to reach a wider audience interested in your products. Promoted Pins enable businesses to boost the visibility of their product pins by targeting specific demographics, interests, or keywords, maximizing exposure and driving traffic to the product listings.

Maintain transparency and credibility by ensuring accurate product information, pricing, and shipping details in your Buyable Pins. Clear and transparent communication builds trust with users, encouraging them to make informed purchasing decisions confidently.

Regularly update product listings and product pins to keep the content fresh, relevant, and engaging for users. Introduce new products, showcase seasonal offers, or highlight best-selling items to maintain user interest and encourage repeat visits to your product boards.

Engage with your audience by responding to inquiries, comments, or feedback related to the products showcased on Pinterest. Promptly address queries, provide additional information, or offer support to enhance user experience and foster a positive relationship with potential customers.

Monitor the performance of Buyable Pins and product listings using Pinterest analytics to gain insights into their effectiveness. Track metrics such as impressions, clicks, saves, and conversion rates to evaluate user engagement and the success of your product-selling strategy. Analyzing this data helps in understanding user preferences, optimizing product listings, and refining your approach for better results.

Consider leveraging Pinterest's expanded shopping features, such as Shopping Spotlights or Shopping List Pins, to showcase curated collections or featured products. These features offer additional opportunities to highlight specific product lines, seasonal promotions, or curated selections, enhancing user engagement and driving sales.

In conclusion, utilizing Pinterest's shopping features, particularly Buyable Pins, offers businesses a powerful platform to showcase and sell products directly to users. By leveraging visually compelling images, accurate product information, audience targeting, and transparent communication, businesses can create a seamless shopping experience for Pinterest users. Maximizing the potential of Pinterest's shopping functionalities can significantly boost sales, drive traffic to online stores, and establish a strong and profitable presence for businesses within the platform's vast user base.

# Chapter - 11

## 11. **Host Contests or Giveaways:** Organize contests or giveaways to encourage engagement, increase your reach, and attract new followers.

Hosting contests or giveaways on Pinterest is a strategic method to foster engagement, expand reach, and attract new followers. These initiatives create excitement, encourage user participation, and amplify brand visibility, making them valuable tools for businesses looking to boost their presence on the platform.

To kickstart a successful contest or giveaway on Pinterest, define clear objectives that align with your marketing goals. Determine whether you aim to increase brand awareness, grow your follower base, drive traffic to your website, or generate user-generated content. Understanding your goals helps shape the structure and strategy of your contest or giveaway.

Select enticing prizes or rewards that resonate with your target audience and align with your brand. Whether it's product bundles, exclusive merchandise, gift cards, or unique experiences, choose prizes that appeal to your audience's interests and preferences, motivating them to participate.

Decide on the contest or giveaway format that best suits your objectives and resonates with your audience. Common formats include photo contests, caption contests, trivia quizzes, creative challenges, or random prize draws. Tailor the format to encourage active engagement and user participation while adhering to Pinterest's guidelines and policies.

Create eye-catching and informative pins that announce and promote the contest or giveaway. Design visually appealing graphics or images that communicate the contest details, including entry requirements, rules, deadlines, and prize details. Incorporate engaging text overlay and compelling visuals to grab users' attention and prompt them to participate.

Craft a compelling pin description that outlines the contest or giveaway rules, entry instructions, and any additional information participants need to know. Include clear and concise guidelines, such as how to enter, eligibility criteria, submission deadlines, and any specific actions participants must take to qualify.

Ensure compliance with Pinterest's guidelines and legal requirements when organizing contests or giveaways. Clearly state the terms and conditions of the contest, including eligibility, entry rules, prize details, and any necessary disclaimers or disclosures to maintain transparency and legality.

Pin the contest or giveaway pins across multiple boards on your profile to maximize visibility and exposure. Create a dedicated board specifically for the contest or giveaway to centralize all related content, making it easily accessible for users interested in participating.

Promote the contest or giveaway across other social media platforms, newsletters, or your website to reach a wider audience beyond Pinterest. Leverage various marketing channels to amplify the contest's visibility and encourage participation from your existing audience and potential new followers.

Encourage user-generated content by requesting participants to create and submit original content, such as photos, videos, or creative entries related to the contest theme or requirements. User-generated content not only increases engagement but also generates authentic interactions with your brand.

Engage with participants by responding to comments, acknowledging entries, or providing updates throughout the contest or giveaway duration. Interacting with participants fosters a sense of community and encourages ongoing engagement.

Select and announce contest winners or recipients in a transparent and timely manner. Communicate the selection process and criteria used for choosing winners to maintain credibility and transparency with participants.

After the contest or giveaway concludes, follow up with a post-announcement pin to thank participants, highlight winners, or showcase user-generated content. Acknowledge the community's contributions and show appreciation for their engagement.

Evaluate the performance and impact of the contest or giveaway using Pinterest analytics and other tracking tools. Measure metrics such as impressions, engagements, reach, new follower acquisition, and website traffic generated during the campaign. Analyzing these metrics provides insights into the contest's effectiveness and helps in refining future strategies.

In conclusion, hosting contests or giveaways on Pinterest is an effective strategy to drive engagement, expand reach, and attract new followers. By offering enticing prizes, creating engaging content, promoting across multiple channels, encouraging user participation, and maintaining transparency, businesses can leverage contests and giveaways as powerful marketing tools. Effectively executed contests not only boost brand visibility but also foster a sense of community, generating excitement and positive interactions with the audience, ultimately contributing to long-term brand growth and engagement on Pinterest.

# Chapter - 12

12. **Collaborate with Influencers:** Partner with influencers or other businesses in your niche for collaborations, joint boards, or sponsored content to reach a broader audience.

Collaborating with influencers or other businesses within your niche on Pinterest presents a strategic opportunity to expand reach, increase brand exposure, and engage with a broader audience. Partnering with influencers or like-minded businesses allows for collaborations, shared boards, or sponsored content, leveraging their established audiences to amplify your brand's presence.

Identify influencers or businesses that align with your brand values, target audience, and niche interests. Conduct thorough research to identify potential collaborators whose audience demographics, interests, and engagement levels closely match your brand's objectives. Look for influencers or businesses with a substantial and engaged following on Pinterest to maximize the collaboration's impact.

Reach out to potential collaborators via direct messages, emails, or through professional networking platforms. Craft personalized and compelling pitches outlining the collaboration proposal, emphasizing the mutual benefits and shared goals of the partnership. Clearly articulate how the collaboration can add value to both parties and resonate with the audience.

Explore different collaboration opportunities, such as joint boards, shared content creation, sponsored posts, or co-hosted events, tailored to suit the strengths and preferences of the collaborators. For instance, co-creating Pinterest boards where both parties contribute relevant content can introduce your brand to the collaborator's audience while providing valuable content for both audiences.

Collaborate on creating compelling and visually appealing pins that align with both brands' aesthetics, values, and target audience preferences. Design pins that effectively communicate the collaborative effort, incorporating elements of both brands seamlessly and engagingly. Create visually cohesive content that resonates with the shared audience while showcasing the unique strengths of each collaborator.

Utilize Pinterest's Rich Pins or Story Pins to add depth and interactivity to the collaborative content. Rich Pins provide additional context, such as product details or article summaries, directly within the pin, while Story Pins offer a dynamic, multi-page format for storytelling and immersive content experiences.

Consider sponsored content as a collaborative opportunity, where one brand sponsors or promotes the other's products or services within their Pinterest content. Ensure transparency by clearly disclosing any sponsored collaborations or partnerships, and maintaining authenticity and trust with the audience.

Promote collaborative content across various channels, including Pinterest, other social media platforms, websites, newsletters, or blogs, to maximize visibility and engagement. Leverage the collaborators' networks and audiences by cross-promoting the content, allowing it to reach a wider audience interested in both brands.

Engage actively with the collaborator's audience by responding to comments, inquiries, or feedback related to the collaborative content. Engaging with the audience fosters a positive relationship and encourages ongoing interaction, contributing to the success of the collaboration.

Measure the performance and impact of the collaboration using Pinterest analytics and other tracking tools. Monitor metrics such as impressions, engagements, click-through rates, follower growth, and audience demographics to assess the collaboration's effectiveness. Analyzing these metrics provides insights into the collaborative content's reach, engagement levels, and its impact on brand visibility and audience expansion.

Evaluate the success of the collaboration based on the agreed-upon key performance indicators (KPIs) and objectives set at the beginning of the partnership. Reflect on the lessons learned, and identify successful strategies, and areas for improvement to inform future collaborative efforts.

In conclusion, collaborating with influencers or businesses on Pinterest presents an excellent opportunity to expand brand reach, engage with a broader audience, and increase brand visibility. By forging strategic partnerships, creating compelling content, cross-promoting, and engaging actively with the audience, businesses can leverage collaborative efforts to enhance their presence on Pinterest and achieve mutually beneficial outcomes. Effective collaborations contribute to increased brand awareness, audience engagement, and long-term growth opportunities on the platform.

# Chapter - 13

## 13. **Use Pinterest Ads:** Invest in promoted pins to reach a targeted audience and increase the visibility of your content.

Using Pinterest ads, specifically Promoted Pins, is a powerful strategy to amplify brand visibility, reach a targeted audience, and enhance the overall performance of your content on the platform. Promoted Pins enable businesses to invest in paid advertising, ensuring their content reaches a wider audience beyond organic reach and appears prominently in users' feeds, search results, and relevant categories.

To begin, navigate to the Pinterest Ads Manager to create Promoted Pins. Define clear objectives for your campaign, whether it's increasing brand awareness, driving website traffic, boosting sales, or promoting specific products/services. Align these objectives with the content and target audience for the campaign.

Select the type of Promoted Pin that best suits your campaign goals. Pinterest offers various formats, including standard Promoted Pins, Video Pins, Carousel Pins, Shopping Pins, and Story Pins.

Choose a format that aligns with your content strategy and resonates with your audience to maximize engagement.

Identify and define your target audience using Pinterest's robust targeting options. Utilize demographic filters, interests, keywords, shopping behaviours, locations, and device preferences to narrow down and reach a highly specific audience segment that aligns with your campaign goals and target demographics.

Craft visually compelling and informative Promoted Pins that effectively communicate your message, product/service offerings, or brand identity. Design attention-grabbing graphics, high-quality images, or engaging videos that stand out in users' feeds and encourage interaction. Incorporate clear calls-to-action and concise text overlays to prompt users to take desired actions.

Optimize the pin's description and title with relevant keywords to improve search visibility and ensure it appears in users' search results when they explore related topics or keywords. Use compelling and descriptive language that encourages users to engage with the pin and explore further.

Set an appropriate budget and bidding strategy for your Promoted Pins campaign. Determine the maximum bid amount you're willing to pay per engagement (CPE), click (CPC), or thousand impressions (CPM). Monitor the campaign's performance regularly and adjust the budget or bid strategy based on the campaign's progress and goals.

Utilize Pinterest's advanced targeting capabilities, such as retargeting options, to reach users who have previously engaged with your brand or visited your website. Retargeting enables you to reconnect with users who have shown interest in your products or services, increasing the chances of conversion.

Track and measure the performance of your Promoted Pins campaign using Pinterest analytics and conversion tracking tools. Monitor metrics such as impressions, clicks, engagements, click-through rates (CTR), conversions, and return on ad spend (ROAS). Analyzing these metrics provides insights into the campaign's effectiveness, audience response, and ROI.

Optimize your Promoted Pins campaign based on the performance data and insights gathered. Make data-driven decisions to refine targeting, adjust bids, modify creative elements, or experiment with different formats to improve campaign performance and achieve better results.

Test and experiment with A/B testing or split testing different variations of Promoted Pins to identify the most effective elements, such as visuals, messaging, calls-to-action, or targeting options. This iterative approach helps in optimizing campaigns for better engagement and conversions.

Create content that aligns with users' interests, provides value, and resonates with their needs or preferences. Offer informative and inspiring content that users find helpful or relevant to their interests, fostering positive interactions and increasing engagement with your Promoted Pins.

Adhere to Pinterest's best practices and guidelines for advertising to ensure compliance and maximize the effectiveness of your Promoted Pins campaigns. Maintain transparency, avoid misleading information, and follow Pinterest's policies to create a positive user experience and build trust with your audience.

In conclusion, leveraging Pinterest ads, particularly Promoted Pins, is an effective way to increase brand visibility, reach a targeted audience, and drive engagement on the platform. By creating visually appealing content, utilizing advanced targeting options, monitoring campaign performance, and optimizing based on insights, businesses can achieve their advertising goals and maximize the impact of their Pinterest advertising efforts. Investing in Promoted Pins allows brands to expand their reach, drive traffic, and achieve tangible results in line with their marketing objectives.

# Chapter - 14

14. **Create Educational Content:** Share informative and educational content related to your niche to establish authority and build trust with your audience.

Creating educational content on Pinterest is a strategic approach to establishing authority, building trust, and engaging with your audience by sharing informative and valuable content within your niche. Educational content serves as a valuable resource, positioning your brand as a knowledgeable source within the industry while providing users with valuable insights and information.

Identify the specific topics, subjects, or themes within your niche that resonate with your target audience. Conduct thorough research to understand the pain points, interests, and questions your audience may have. Develop a content strategy that addresses these needs and provides solutions, insights, or valuable information.

Utilize various formats to create educational content, including how-to guides, tutorials, infographics, tips, industry insights, statistics, trend analyses, or explainer videos. Choose formats that effectively communicate complex or informative content in a visually appealing and easy-to-understand manner.

Craft visually engaging and informative pins that attract attention and communicate the essence of your educational content. Design graphics, images, or videos that effectively convey the key points of your content. Use clear and concise text overlays, compelling visuals, and branding elements to create impactful pins that stand out in users' feeds.

Incorporate compelling pin descriptions that provide context, summaries, or additional information about the educational content. Use relevant keywords, concise explanations, and calls to action to encourage users to engage further or explore the content in-depth.

Create dedicated boards specifically curated for educational content within your niche. Organize and categorize your educational pins systematically to make it easier for users to find and explore relevant information. Consider segmenting boards based on different topics or levels of expertise to cater to diverse audience interests.

Focus on providing high-quality, accurate, and up-to-date information in your educational content. Ensure that the content is well-researched, credible, and adds genuine value to your audience. Authentic and reliable information fosters trust and credibility, encouraging users to view your brand as a reputable source of knowledge.

Incorporate storytelling or relatable narratives within your educational content to captivate users' attention and make the information more engaging and memorable. Share personal experiences, case studies, success stories, or practical examples to illustrate key points and connect with your audience on a deeper level.

Promote your educational content across various channels, including Pinterest, other social media platforms, newsletters, or blogs, to maximize its visibility and reach. Leverage different marketing channels to amplify the educational content's exposure and attract a wider audience interested in learning within your niche.

Engage actively with your audience by responding to comments, questions, or feedback related to your educational content. Encourage discussions, provide additional insights, or address queries to foster a community of learning and interaction around your content.

Regularly assess the performance of your educational content using Pinterest analytics and other tracking tools. Monitor metrics such as impressions, saves, clicks, engagement rates, and comments to gauge the content's effectiveness and audience response. Analyzing this data helps in understanding which topics or formats resonate best with your audience.

Continuously refine and update your educational content strategy based on audience feedback, evolving trends, or emerging topics within your niche. Stay informed about industry developments and adapt your content strategy to provide timely and relevant information to your audience.

In conclusion, creating educational content on Pinterest is a valuable strategy to establish authority, build trust, and engage with your audience by sharing valuable insights and information within your niche. By creating visually appealing, informative, and credible content, businesses can position themselves as thought leaders, nurturing a loyal audience base and fostering a positive brand reputation on the platform. Educational content serves as a powerful tool to educate, inspire, and connect with users, ultimately contributing to long-term brand growth and engagement on Pinterest.

# Chapter - 15

15. **Offer Consultation or Services:** Promote your services or expertise by creating pins that showcase what you offer and how it benefits potential clients.

Promoting your services or expertise on Pinterest is an effective way to showcase your offerings, attract potential clients, and highlight the value you bring to your audience. By creating compelling pins that effectively communicate what you offer and how it benefits potential clients, you can establish credibility, generate leads, and drive business growth.

Identify and define the specific services or expertise you want to promote on Pinterest. Whether it's consulting services, professional expertise, coaching programs, creative services, or any other offerings, clearly articulate the value proposition and benefits that clients can gain from working with you.

Craft visually captivating and informative pins that effectively represent your services or expertise. Design high-quality graphics, images, or videos that showcase your offerings in a visually appealing manner. Use clear and concise text overlays, compelling visuals, and branding elements to communicate key messages and entice users to learn more.

Incorporate compelling pin descriptions that highlight the unique aspects of your services or expertise. Use persuasive language, relevant keywords, and specific details to convey the value, benefits, and outcomes clients can expect by engaging with your services. Include clear calls-to-action that encourage users to take the next step, such as visiting your website, contacting you, or exploring more information.

Create dedicated boards specifically curated to showcase your services, expertise, or case studies. Organize and categorize your pins strategically to make it easy for users to navigate and explore your offerings. Consider creating separate boards for different services or aspects of your expertise to cater to diverse client interests.

Utilize Pinterest's Rich Pins or Story Pins to provide additional context, information, or details about your services directly within the pin. Rich Pins can include real-time updates on pricing, availability, or specific details about the services, while Story Pins offers a dynamic, multi-page format for storytelling and immersive content experiences.

Share client testimonials, success stories, or case studies through your pins to showcase the results and positive experiences of working with you. Authentic testimonials and real-life examples of your expertise or services' impact can significantly influence potential clients and build trust in your abilities.

Offer value through educational content related to your services or expertise. Create informative pins, how-to guides, tips, or resources that provide valuable insights, information, or solutions within your niche. Educating your audience not only showcases your knowledge but also positions you as a helpful resource, fostering trust and credibility.

Promote your services or expertise across various marketing channels, including Pinterest, other social media platforms, your website, newsletters, or blogs. Leverage different platforms to amplify the reach of your offerings, targeting audiences interested in your niche and services.

Engage actively with your audience by responding to comments, inquiries, or messages related to your services or expertise. Promptly address queries, provide additional information, or offer support to potential clients, fostering a positive interaction and demonstrating your commitment to client satisfaction.

Use Pinterest analytics and tracking tools to monitor the performance of your service-related pins and boards. Track metrics such as impressions, clicks, saves, engagement rates, and conversions to evaluate the effectiveness of your service promotion efforts. Analyzing this data helps in understanding user behaviour and optimizing your strategy for better results.

Collaborate with influencers or partner with complementary businesses to expand the reach of your service promotions on Pinterest. Collaborative efforts can introduce your services to new audiences and provide opportunities for cross-promotion, increasing visibility and attracting potential clients.

Continuously refine and update your service promotion strategy based on audience feedback, market trends, or changes within your niche. Stay informed about industry developments, adjust your messaging, and adapt your offerings to meet the evolving needs of potential clients.

In conclusion, leveraging Pinterest to promote your services or expertise involves creating visually appealing and informative content that effectively communicates your value proposition and benefits to potential clients. By showcasing your offerings through compelling pins, providing valuable information, sharing testimonials, and engaging with your audience, you can establish credibility, generate interest, and attract potential clients to explore and engage with your services. Effectively promoting your services on Pinterest serves as a powerful tool for expanding your client base, fostering trust, and driving business growth.

# Chapter - 16

16. **Curate Curiosity Boards:** Create boards that pique interest and curiosity, driving users to explore and engage with your content.

Curating curiosity boards on Pinterest involves creating visually stimulating and intriguing boards that captivate users' interest, encouraging them to explore and engage with your content. These boards aim to spark curiosity, draw attention, and evoke a sense of fascination, compelling users to delve deeper into your curated content.

Here's a comprehensive guide to creating curiosity boards on Pinterest:

1. **Identify Themes or Topics of Interest:**

Determine specific themes, topics, or subjects that align with your audience's interests. These could include niche hobbies, intriguing facts, mind-bending trivia, unique art forms, historical mysteries, futuristic concepts, or anything that sparks curiosity and captivates the imagination.

2. **Craft Captivating Board Titles:**
Create board titles that evoke curiosity and intrigue. Use catchy, enigmatic, or thought-provoking titles that entice users to explore further. For instance, "Unsolved Mysteries of History," "Intriguing Facts You Didn't Know," or "Explore the Wonders of the Universe."

3. **Curate High-Quality and Diverse Content:**
Populate your curiosity boards with high-quality and diverse content that aligns with the board's theme. Curate a mix of visually engaging images, infographics, intriguing facts, thought-provoking quotes, or captivating videos that stimulate curiosity and encourage exploration.

4. **Utilize Visually Compelling Pins:**
Design visually compelling and attention-grabbing pins that represent the essence of your curated content. Use captivating visuals, bold imagery, striking colours, and intriguing graphics to stand out in users' feeds and entice them to delve deeper into your boards.

5. **Create Engaging Pin Descriptions:**
Craft pin descriptions that complement the visuals and evoke curiosity. Use descriptive and compelling language that prompts users to explore further. Incorporate intriguing teasers, questions, or snippets of information to pique interest and encourage engagement.

6. **Organize Boards Creatively:**

Organize your boards in a visually appealing and organized manner. Arrange pins strategically within boards to create an aesthetic flow that maintains users' interest and encourages them to explore more content.

7. **Tell a Story or Create a Narrative:**
   Develop a storytelling approach within your boards. Arrange pins in a sequential or thematic order that tells a compelling narrative, reveals mysteries step-by-step, or uncovers fascinating facts, captivating users and compelling them to keep exploring.

8. **Offer Exclusive or Unusual Content:**
   Provide exclusive or less commonly known information, behind-the-scenes insights, or unique perspectives within your curated content. Offering something novel or exclusive encourages users to engage more deeply with your content.

9. **Encourage Exploration and Interaction:**
   Encourage users to interact with your curiosity boards by inviting them to share their thoughts, theories, or additional information related to the content. Engage with users who comment or interact with your pins to foster a sense of community and exploration.

10. **Promote Across Multiple Channels:**
   Promote your curiosity boards across various platforms, including Pinterest, other social media channels, your website, blogs, or newsletters. Share intriguing snippets or teasers to attract users to explore your Pinterest boards further.

11. **Measure Performance and Adapt Strategy:**
   Use Pinterest analytics and tracking tools to monitor the performance of your curiosity boards. Track metrics like impressions, clicks, saves, and engagement rates to evaluate the boards' effectiveness. Adapt your strategy based on insights and user interactions for continued improvement.

12. **Collaborate and Expand Reach:**
   Collaborate with influencers or partner with complementary brands or content creators to expand the reach of your curiosity boards. Collaborations introduce your boards to new audiences and provide opportunities for cross-promotion, increasing visibility and engagement.

13. **Refine and Update Strategy:**
   Continuously refine your strategy based on audience feedback, trends, or emerging topics. Stay adaptable and experiment with new content formats, themes, or storytelling techniques to keep your curiosity boards fresh and engaging.

In summary, creating curiosity boards on Pinterest involves curating visually appealing and intriguing content that sparks users' interest and drives engagement. By crafting captivating visuals, using compelling descriptions, telling stories, offering exclusive content, and encouraging interaction, you can create an immersive experience that encourages users to explore and engage with your curated content. Effectively curating curiosity boards helps in building a loyal audience, fostering exploration, and establishing your brand as a source of intriguing and captivating content on Pinterest.

# Chapter -17

## 17. **Share User-Generated Content:** Encourage users to share their experiences with your products or services and feature their content on your boards.

Encouraging user-generated content (UGC) on Pinterest involves inviting users to share their experiences, stories, or creative content related to your products or services. Featuring this UGC on your boards not only amplifies engagement but also builds a sense of community around your brand. Here's a comprehensive guide on how to effectively share user-generated content on Pinterest:

1. **Establish Guidelines and Encourage Participation:**
   Clearly define guidelines for users to create and share content related to your brand. Encourage them to share their experiences, testimonials, photos, or creative expressions involving your products or services. Provide instructions or prompts that inspire users to participate.

2. **Create a Dedicated Hashtag or Campaign:**
   Develop a unique and catchy hashtag or campaign name that users can use when sharing their content. This helps in tracking and curating user-generated content easily. Promote the hashtag across your social media channels, website, and Pinterest to encourage participation.

3. **Feature UGC on Specific Boards:**
   Create dedicated Pinterest boards specifically curated to showcase user-generated content. Organize and feature the UGC in these boards, allowing users to see their contributions

highlighted. Consider different boards for diverse types of content, such as testimonials, photos, or creative interpretations.

4. **Engage and Acknowledge Contributors:**
   Actively engage with users who contribute to UGC by acknowledging their submissions, liking, commenting, or repinning their content. Show appreciation for their contributions by responding positively to their posts, which encourages further engagement and participation.

5. **Encourage Diverse Content Formats:**
   Encourage users to share diverse content formats, including photos, videos, testimonials, stories, how-to guides, or creative interpretations. This variety adds depth and richness to your boards, showcasing diverse user experiences and perspectives.

6. **Highlight UGC Stories and Testimonials:**
   Feature compelling user stories, testimonials, or reviews on your Pinterest boards. Curate these in a visually appealing manner, incorporating visuals and text overlays to highlight the user experience or sentiment associated with your brand.

7. **Leverage Rich Pins for UGC:**
   Use Pinterest's Rich Pins to enhance UGC visibility. Enable article, product, or recipe-rich pins to provide additional context and details within the pins. This additional information can make user-generated content more informative and engaging.

8. **Collaborate with Contributors:**
   Collaborate with users who consistently contribute high-quality UGC. Feature them in collaborative boards or highlight their content in special showcases. Building relationships with active contributors strengthens brand loyalty and fosters a sense of community.

9. **Promote UGC Across Channels:**

Promote UGC across multiple platforms, including Pinterest, social media, newsletters, and your website. Showcase user-generated content snippets or teasers to encourage more users to contribute and engage.

10. **Create UGC Campaigns or Contests:**
Organize UGC campaigns or contests to incentivize users to create and share content. Offer rewards, recognition, or exclusive features for outstanding contributions. This encourages more users to participate and generates a buzz around your brand.

11. **Ensure Consent and Rights Management:**
Respect users' rights and privacy by ensuring that contributors provide consent for the use of their content. Implement clear guidelines regarding content ownership and usage rights when users share their content.

12. **Monitor Performance and User Engagement:**
Utilize Pinterest analytics to track the performance of UGC boards. Monitor metrics such as engagement rates, shares, and comments to gauge the effectiveness of UGC campaigns. Analyzing this data provides insights into the content that resonates most with your audience.

13. **Express Gratitude and Recognition:**
Continuously express gratitude and recognition to users who contribute to UGC. Highlight outstanding contributions, feature active participants, and publicly acknowledge their creativity and support.

14. **Reinforce Community Engagement:**
Encourage discussions and interactions among users by fostering a sense of community around UGC. Respond to comments, prompt conversations, and encourage users to engage with each other to create a vibrant community space.

15. **Continuously Refresh and Curate UGC Boards:**
    Regularly update UGC boards with fresh content to maintain user interest and engagement. Rotate featured content to showcase a variety of contributions and keep the boards dynamic.

In summary, leveraging user-generated content on Pinterest involves actively engaging users to contribute and share their experiences related to your brand. By curating UGC boards, acknowledging contributors, promoting diverse content formats, and fostering a vibrant community, you can create an immersive and engaging environment that strengthens brand loyalty and amplifies engagement around your products or services. Effectively leveraging UGC on Pinterest contributes to building a loyal customer base and fostering a sense of belonging within your brand community.

# Chapter - 18

18. **Cross-Promote on Other Platforms:** Share your pins on other social media platforms, blogs, or websites to drive traffic back to your Pinterest account.

Cross-promoting your Pinterest content on other platforms is a powerful strategy to expand your reach, drive traffic to your Pinterest account, and increase engagement with your pins. Leveraging various platforms to showcase your Pinterest content widens your audience and encourages users across different channels to explore and engage with your pins. Here's a comprehensive guide on effectively cross-promoting your Pinterest content:

1. **Identify Cross-Promotion Channels:**
   Determine the social media platforms, blogs, websites, newsletters, or other online channels where your target audience is active. These platforms can include Facebook, Instagram, Twitter, LinkedIn, blogs, or industry-specific websites.

2. **Create Compelling Pins:**
   Craft visually appealing and informative pins on Pinterest that effectively represent your content. Design attention-grabbing graphics, high-quality images, or engaging videos with clear and concise text overlays that encourage users to explore further.

3. **Utilize Pin Descriptions Effectively:**
   Write compelling pin descriptions that complement your visuals. Use relevant keywords, persuasive language, and calls to action to prompt users to engage with your pins. Ensure that descriptions are concise and informative, enticing users to click and explore.

4. **Share Pins on Social Media Platforms:**
   Share your Pinterest pins on various social media platforms where your audience is active. Repurpose your pins by posting them on Facebook, Twitter, Instagram, LinkedIn, or other relevant platforms. Include a brief description and a link to your Pinterest board or pin.

5. **Utilize Stories and Reels on Instagram:**
   Leverage Instagram's Stories and Reels features to share your Pinterest content. Create short, engaging videos or image slideshows using your pins and direct your Instagram audience to your Pinterest profile or specific pins.

6. **Pin Your Content on Pinterest Group Boards:**

Join and actively participate in relevant group boards on Pinterest. Pin your content to these boards, expanding its visibility to a broader audience interested in specific topics or niches.

7. **Embed Pins on Websites or Blogs:**
Embed your Pinterest pins directly into your website or blog posts. Incorporate pins related to your content or articles, allowing website visitors to engage with your Pinterest content without leaving your site.

8. **Promote Pins in Newsletters:**
Include highlights or snippets of your Pinterest content in newsletters sent to your subscribers. Add pins with brief descriptions and links to drive recipients to explore your Pinterest boards or specific pins.

9. **Collaborate with Influencers or Partners:**
Collaborate with influencers or partner with complementary brands to cross-promote your Pinterest content. Encourage influencers to share your pins with their followers, expanding your reach to their audience.

10. **Optimize Posts for Each Platform:**
Tailor your content for each platform based on its unique audience preferences and formats. Customize captions, hashtags, or descriptions to align with the tone and style of each platform while maintaining consistency in messaging.

11. **Create Cross-Promotion Campaigns:**
Develop cross-promotion campaigns across multiple channels, synchronizing your content releases for maximum impact. Run coordinated campaigns where content is shared simultaneously across platforms to generate buzz and engagement.

12. **Monitor Performance and Adjust Strategy:**

Track the performance of your cross-promotion efforts using analytics tools available on different platforms. Monitor metrics such as click-through rates, engagement rates, traffic sources, and conversions. Analyze this data to refine your cross-promotion strategy and focus on channels driving the most traffic and engagement.

13. **Engage with Audiences Across Platforms:**
   Actively engage with audiences on different platforms by responding to comments, messages, or inquiries related to your content. Foster conversations, answer questions and encourage users to explore further by interacting with your pins.

14. **Schedule Content for Optimal Timing:**
   Schedule your cross-promotion content at times when your audience is most active on each platform. Utilize scheduling tools to ensure your Pinterest content reaches users when they are more likely to engage.

15. **Experiment with Different Formats:**
   Experiment with various content formats, such as images, videos, infographics, or carousels, across different platforms to determine what resonates best with your audience on each platform.

In summary, cross-promoting your Pinterest content on other platforms involves leveraging various online channels to showcase your pins, drive traffic back to your Pinterest account, and engage users across multiple touchpoints. By strategically sharing and repurposing your Pinterest content on social media, websites, newsletters, and collaborative efforts, you can amplify your reach, attract new audiences, and encourage deeper engagement with your Pinterest pins, ultimately contributing to increased visibility and growth on the platform.

# Chapter - 19

19. **Create Seasonal or Holiday Boards:**
Capitalize on seasonal trends or holidays by
creating themed boards and pins to attract
seasonal shoppers.

Creating seasonal or holiday-themed boards on Pinterest is an
excellent strategy to capitalize on specific periods, events, or festive
occasions throughout the year. These themed boards and pins
allow businesses to align with seasonal trends or holidays, attract
seasonal shoppers, and engage with audiences looking for related
content. Here's a comprehensive guide on effectively creating
seasonal or holiday boards on Pinterest:

1. **Identify Seasonal or Holiday Themes:**
   Recognize key seasonal periods or holidays relevant to your
niche or industry. These could include traditional holidays like
Christmas, Valentine's Day, Halloween, or specific seasons like
summer, winter, back-to-school, or events like Black Friday,
Mother's Day, or Earth Day.

2. **Plan Content Calendar for Seasonal Boards:**
   Create a content calendar outlining the seasonal or
holiday-themed content you intend to showcase on Pinterest. Plan
to curate and publish pins aligned with each specific occasion or
seasonal trend.

3. **Craft Seasonal and Festive Pins:**
   Design visually appealing, themed pins that resonate with the
seasonal or holiday spirit. Use vibrant colours, festive imagery,

themed decorations, or seasonal elements relevant to the occasion to capture users' attention.

4. **Develop Seasonal Boards:**
   Create dedicated Pinterest boards for each seasonal or holiday theme. Organize your boards based on different holidays or seasonal events, allowing users to explore specific content related to each occasion.

5. **Curate Diverse Content:**
   Populate your seasonal boards with a variety of content formats such as DIY ideas, gift guides, recipes, decoration tips, fashion trends, holiday activities, or event planning suggestions. Ensure diverse content that caters to various interests within the seasonal theme.

6. **Utilize Rich Pins for Seasonal Content:**
   Enable Rich Pins such as product, recipe, or article pins for your seasonal content. Rich Pins provide additional information directly on the pin, making it more valuable and enticing for users seeking specific details related to the season or holiday.

7. **Highlight Seasonal Promotions or Offers:**
   Showcase seasonal discounts, special offers, or limited-time promotions on your themed boards. Create pins that highlight these promotions to attract users looking for holiday deals or exclusive seasonal offers.

8. **Collaborate with Influencers or Partners:**
   Collaborate with influencers or partner with other brands or content creators to cross-promote seasonal content. Engage in joint boards, campaigns, or collaborations to expand the reach of your seasonal pins and boards.

9. **Share DIY or How-To Guides:**

Offer helpful DIY guides, tutorials, or how-to content relevant to the season or holiday. Provide step-by-step instructions or creative ideas that users can implement during the festive period or seasonal celebrations.

10. **Pin Early and Plan Ahead:**
Start pinning seasonal content ahead of time to maximize its visibility before the holiday or seasonal peak. Plan and schedule pins in advance to ensure timely delivery and engagement.

11. **Encourage Engagement and Interaction:**
Prompt users to engage with your seasonal content by encouraging comments, sharing experiences, or asking for suggestions. Foster a sense of community around the seasonal theme, encouraging users to interact with your boards and each other.

12. **Promote Seasonal Boards Across Channels:**
Promote your seasonal boards across various marketing channels, including social media, websites, newsletters, or blogs. Share snippets, teasers, or highlights to attract users to explore your themed boards on Pinterest.

13. **Monitor Performance and Adapt Strategy:**
Use Pinterest analytics to track the performance of your seasonal boards and pins. Analyze metrics such as engagement rates, click-throughs, and saves to understand which seasonal content resonates most with your audience. Adjust your strategy based on the insights gathered.

14. **Stay Authentic and Relevant:**
Ensure that your seasonal content aligns with your brand's identity and remains relevant to your audience. Maintain authenticity while incorporating seasonal themes to captivate users without deviating from your brand image.

15. **Evaluate and Refine Strategy:**
   After each seasonal event or holiday, evaluate the performance of your themed boards. Identify successes, learn from challenges, and refine your strategy for future seasonal campaigns based on the outcomes.

In summary, leveraging seasonal or holiday-themed boards on Pinterest involves strategically curating themed content, creating engaging pins, and offering valuable resources aligned with specific occasions or trends. By planning, creating diverse content formats, utilizing Rich Pins, and promoting across channels, businesses can attract seasonal shoppers, engage audiences, and drive traffic by capitalizing on seasonal trends and festive occasions throughout the year. This approach allows brands to remain relevant, foster user engagement, and expand their reach during key seasonal periods or holidays.

# Chapter - 20

20. **Track Analytics and Optimize:** Monitor Pinterest analytics to understand what content performs best and use this data to refine your strategies for better results.

Monitoring Pinterest analytics is crucial for understanding the performance of your content, identifying trends, and optimizing strategies to achieve better results. Utilizing these insights helps in refining your Pinterest marketing efforts, enhancing engagement, and maximizing the impact of your pins and boards. Here is a comprehensive guide on tracking analytics and optimizing strategies on Pinterest:

1. **Accessing Pinterest Analytics:**
   Pinterest offers a built-in analytics tool available to business accounts. Access your analytics dashboard by clicking on your profile picture and selecting "Analytics" from the drop-down menu. This dashboard provides valuable data on pin performance, audience demographics, and engagement metrics.

2. **Understanding Analytics Metrics:**
   Familiarize yourself with key metrics provided in Pinterest analytics:
   - Impressions: The number of times your pins have been seen by users.
   - Saves: The number of times users have saved your pins to their boards.
   - Clicks: The number of times users clicked through to view your content.
   - Engagements: The total interactions (e.g., clicks, saves, close-ups) on your pins.
   - Audience Insights: Demographic information about your audience, including interests, location, and device usage.

3. **Identifying Top-Performing Content:**
   Analyze your pins to identify top-performing content based on engagement, clicks, and saves. Pay attention to which pins receive the most engagement and what content resonates best with your audience.

4. **Pin Performance Analysis:**
   Review the performance of individual pins to understand which visuals, descriptions, or formats drive the highest engagement. Identify trends in content types, topics, or styles that perform exceptionally well.

5. **Board Analytics Review:**
   Evaluate the performance of your Pinterest boards. Identify which boards attract the most engagement, which ones require improvement, and which themes or categories resonate most with your audience.

6. **Audience Insights Utilization:**
   Utilize audience insights to understand your audience demographics, interests, and behaviour. This information helps in tailoring content to better match the preferences of your audience.

7. **Tracking Clicks and Referral Traffic:**
   Monitor the number of clicks on your pins and their subsequent referral traffic to your website. Identify which pins drive the most traffic and conversions, enabling you to focus on content that generates the most value.

8. **A/B Testing and Experimentation:**
   Conduct A/B tests by creating variations of pins or boards to test different visuals, descriptions, or formats. Analyze the performance of these variations to understand what resonates best with your audience.

9. **Optimizing Pin Descriptions and Keywords:**
   Use analytics insights to optimize pin descriptions and keywords. Incorporate keywords and phrases that resonate well with your audience, increasing the discoverability of your pins in Pinterest search results.

10. **Content Calendar Adjustments:**
    Refine your content calendar based on analytics data. Focus on creating more content aligned with the themes, topics, or formats that perform well and resonate with your audience.

11. **Frequency and Timing Analysis:**
    Analyze the best times and frequency for pinning. Determine when your audience is most active and engaged, and adjust your pinning schedule accordingly for maximum impact.

12. **Promoted Pins Performance Review:**
    If using promoted pins, track their performance closely. Evaluate the return on investment (ROI) and adjust targeting, budget, or content based on analytics data to optimize campaigns.

13. **Continuous Monitoring and Iteration:**
    Regularly review analytics data and make iterative adjustments to your strategies. Pinterest trends and user preferences may change over time, requiring ongoing optimization.

14. **Benchmarking and Goal Setting:**
    Set measurable goals based on analytics insights. Benchmark your performance against these goals and continuously strive to improve key metrics such as engagement rates, clicks, or conversions.

15. **Integration with Overall Marketing Strategy:**
    Integrate Pinterest analytics data with your overall marketing strategy. Use insights gained from Pinterest analytics to inform and optimize your broader digital marketing efforts.

In summary, leveraging Pinterest analytics involves a comprehensive review and analysis of your pins, boards, audience behaviour, and performance metrics. By consistently tracking analytics, identifying top-performing content, understanding audience preferences, and optimizing strategies based on data-driven insights, businesses can refine their Pinterest marketing approaches, enhance engagement, and achieve better results on the platform. This iterative process of analyzing, optimizing, and adapting strategies based on analytics is essential for continual improvement and maximizing the effectiveness of your Pinterest marketing efforts.

# Author Introduction:

**Introduction to P Adhil Khan: Bringing in Cash on Pinterest**

P Adhil Khan, a distinguished authority in digital marketing and an accomplished author, presents a comprehensive roadmap in his latest book, "Bringing in Cash on Pinterest: A Step-by-Step Guide." With an extensive background in online commerce and a particular focus on leveraging social media platforms for financial success, Khan's insights offer invaluable guidance for individuals and businesses aiming to monetize their presence on Pinterest.

In this step-by-step guide, Khan shares a wealth of knowledge gained through years of expertise in digital entrepreneurship and marketing. His strategies are tailored to harness the immense potential of Pinterest as a lucrative platform for driving sales, increasing brand visibility, and maximizing revenue streams.

Khan's approachable and actionable advice empowers readers, whether entrepreneurs, marketers, or aspiring influencers, to navigate the dynamic landscape of Pinterest. By delving into proven techniques, innovative strategies, and practical tips, he equips readers with the tools needed to effectively monetize their presence on this visual discovery platform.

Through his methodical breakdown of Pinterest's functionalities, optimization techniques, and monetization strategies, Khan offers a roadmap that takes readers on a journey from novice pinners to savvy marketers. His emphasis on a structured approach, accompanied by real-world examples and case studies, ensures that readers gain a deep understanding of the platform's potential and how to harness it for financial gain.

For anyone seeking to transform their Pinterest presence into a revenue-generating asset, P Adhil Khan's "Bringing in Cash on Pinterest: A Step-by-Step Guide" stands as an indispensable resource. With Khan's guidance, readers are poised to unlock the full monetary potential of Pinterest and cultivate a successful online business or brand.